If you love making things, then this book's got all the ideas you need – just follow the numbered steps and photographs. You'll find most of the materials you need around the home or in most shops, but if you haven't got exactly what's shown, then use whatever you can find. There's no right or wrong way to make anything so get stuck in and use your imagination! Look out for the paint splats, too, which give you handy hints to make your art extra SMart!

FAKE FISH TANK

YOU WILL NEED

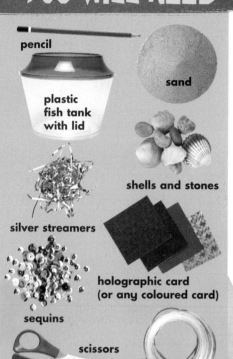

pencil

sand

plastic fish tank with lid

shells and stones

silver streamers

holographic card (or any coloured card)

sequins

scissors

clear thread or fishing line

glue stick

tape

green pipe cleaners

green soft modelling clay

Make the perfect pets by filling a fish tank with pretty paper fish.

1

Start by putting a layer of sand in the bottom of the tank, about 2cm thick. Then arrange some shells and stones on the sand.

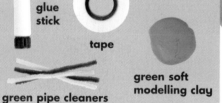

2

Twist the pipe cleaners by wrapping them around a pencil. Then push one end of each pipe cleaner into a lump of modelling clay.

3 Trace this fish shape onto card and cut it out to make a template. Fold a piece of holographic card in half and draw round the template on one side. Cut it out to make two fish shapes.

Cut a 12cm length of clear thread. Place it between the two fish shapes, then glue them together to hold it in place.

4 Make about five different coloured fish and decorate both sides. Add stripes to the tail and stick on card and sequin eyes.

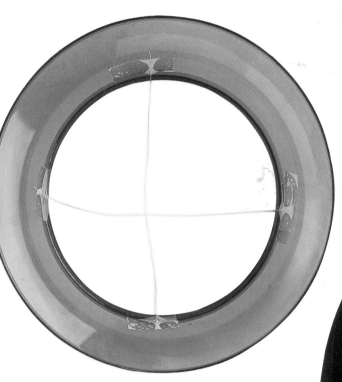

5 Cut two lengths of clear thread, about 3cm longer than the diameter of the fish tank lid. Tape them across the lid in a cross shape.

6 Attach the fish to the lid, tying them to the cross of thread so that they are all different lengths. Tie on some silver streamers too. ➪

Make modelling clay creatures to add to your tank. You could even try making a mini treasure chest or a bridge as well.

7

Place the pieces of pipe cleaner seaweed inside the tank. Carefully lower the lid into place, moving the seaweed if necessary to fit the fish around it.

QUICK MAKE BACK SCRUBBER

YOU WILL NEED

- colourful body puff
- wooden spoon
- scissors
- strong waterproof glue
- white, black and red foam
- kitchen cloth

Keep yourself scrubbed clean with this colourful clown.

1

Cut out the eyes, nose and mouth from the foam and glue them to the front of the wooden spoon. Glue the body puff to the back of the spoon.

2

Cut a bow tie from the kitchen cloth and glue it to the top of the spoon handle.

Look for strong, waterproof glue in hardware and DIY shops.

BATHING

empty margarine tub, deep with rounded sides

long, thin chocolate biscuit

chocolate muffin

tube of red icing

blue or green jelly

paper cake case

silver cake decoration balls

round chocolate biscuit

paintbrush

desiccated coconut

blue and white paint

small jelly sweet

strawberry and cola sweet laces

1

Paint the margarine tub light blue. Make the jelly, following the instructions on the packet. Pour it into the tub so it is about two thirds full, then leave it to set.

2

Break the ends off the long chocolate biscuit and poke them into the jelly to make feet. Spoon out some of the jelly and drop the muffin in the hole to make the body.

3

Push two silver balls into the round biscuit to make eyes. Now pipe on a mouth and two rosy cheeks with the tube icing. Plait three lengths of strawberry lace to make hair.

4

Carefully balance the head on top of the body, using a small blob of tube icing to 'glue' it on if necessary. Place two short pieces of cola lace beside the body to make arms.

BEAUTY

5 Place the cake case on the head. Sprinkle desiccated coconut onto the jelly 'water' and drop in the jelly sweet 'soap'.

If you've got a tube of chocolate icing, you can pipe on eyebrows, too.

VALENTINE SURPRISE

empty stock cube box

pink, red and purple paper, card and tissue paper

black and pink felt-tip pens

scissors

double-sided tape

sparkly pipe cleaner

glue stick

sequins

paintbrush

lilac paint

Surprise someone with a pop-up Valentine's message.

1 First cut lots of different sized heart shapes from the paper, card and tissue paper.

2 Paint the box all over. When it is dry, glue the heart shapes onto it. Add some sequins and draw on felt-tip pen swirls too.

10

4

Cut a large heart from pink paper and write your message on it. Loosely coil the pipe cleaner around your finger to make a spiral, then glue the heart to one end.

Be mine!

3

Cut two strips of card about 3cm x 60cm. Glue them together to make a right angle. Now fold one colour over the other to make a concertina.

5

Attach the pipe cleaner to one end of the card concertina with double-sided tape. Now put some double-sided tape on the other end of the concertina.

6

Drop the concertina into the box and press it in place. Carefully fold the concertina and pipe cleaner into the box. Shut the lid so your message is ready to burst out.

CROCODILE RACK

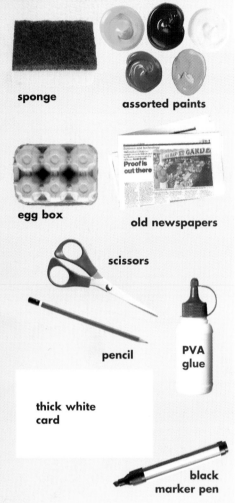

- sponge
- assorted paints
- egg box
- old newspapers
- scissors
- pencil
- PVA glue
- thick white card
- black marker pen

This crocodile's perfect for keeping your CDs or computer disks in order.

1 Draw a crocodile shape onto the card, about 75cm in length from nose to tail. Cut it out. Draw round the crocodile shape on another piece of card and cut that out too. Draw on the crocodile's face, as shown.

2 Cut a strip of card 14cm wide and 120cm long. Fold it every 12cm to make a concertina.

3 Tear the newspaper into small rectangles. Glue the rectangles onto the two crocodile shapes, overlapping them to look like scales.

4 Dip the sponge into green paint and dab it onto both sides of the two crocodile shapes and the concertina of card. Use different colours to shade the crocodile.

5 Cut out two sections of the egg box to make eyes. Paint each eye green and draw on a pupil. Glue one eye to each side of the crocodile. Then add some teeth cut from white card and nostrils cut from card and painted black.

6 Put some PVA glue along one edge of the card concertina and stick it to the inside of one crocodile shape. Then glue the second crocodile shape to the other side of the concertina.

The joy of clay is that you can mould it into almost anything. Whether you're using soft non-hardening clay, air-drying clay or oven-bake clay, here are some ideas to get you started.

This apple and cat are made from coloured **soft non-hardening clay**. Make the apple shape first, then gently press on the leaves, stalk and worm details.

Make the cat's basic body shape first, then build up the different coloured layers. Press on the stripes, claws and the features on the face. Use your fingers to 'smudge' colours together, like the fur on the cat's chest.

You can turn clay creations into something useful, like this fish keyring and personalised door plate, both made from **air-drying clay**. Make the hole in the top with a sharp pencil while the clay's still wet, then paint it when it is dry.

To get smooth curves on this dinosaur made from **air-drying clay**, dip your fingers in water and run them over the clay. Air-drying clay takes about 24 hours to dry out. Wait until it's completely dry before painting it with either acrylic or poster paints, then add a coat of clear varnish over the dry paint.

Roll **air-drying clay** to a thickness of about 1cm and cut out a square tile shape. Decorate the tile by sticking smaller pieces of clay onto the wet tile with water, or by scraping a pattern into the surface of the wet tile. The noughts and crosses game is just four strips stuck onto the tile. The separate counters are also made from air-drying clay, painted with an O on one side and an X on the other.

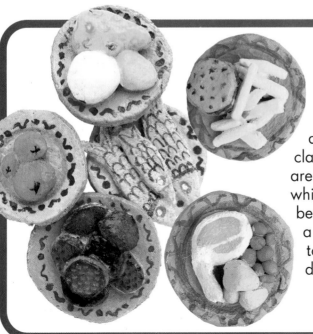

Make mini plates of food from any type of clay. If you are using clay which needs to be painted, use a thin brush to get the details right.

Work with clay on a smooth, clean and cool surface. Lift it occasionally as you work to make sure it isn't sticking.

15

SHOE FACES

fur fabric

string of sequins

paintbrush

red and white acrylic paint

white card

black card

glitter glue or spray

googly eyes

trainer (without the lace)

PVA glue

scissors

Got an old trainer lying around? Then turn it into a funky face!

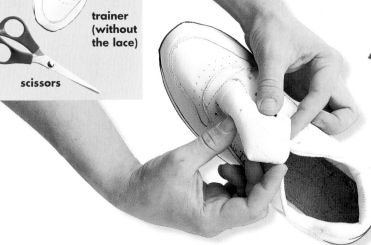

1 Pull out the tongue of the trainer. Turn it into a nose by pinching it together underneath and folding the end under to make nostrils. Use glue to hold it in the nose shape, then glue it down onto the trainer.

2 Pull out the insole, then paint the trainer a skin colour. You might need more than one coat. Paint inside and around the heel red to make the mouth and lips.

Cut off the end of the insole and paint it red to make a tongue.

3 Cut two rows of teeth from white card. Make each row long enough to go round one side of the mouth. Then make a pair of eyelashes from black card, as shown.

4 Decorate the eyelashes with glitter glue and leave them to dry. Then glue the googly eyes and eyelashes in place.

5 Glue both rows of teeth in place behind the lips. Push the tongue into position and glue that, too.

6 Cut the fur fabric into a strip and glue it around the top of the trainer to make the hair. Decorate the hair with glitter glue or spray. ⇨

7

Now add any final decorations. A sequin hairband completes the glam look of this shoe face.

With a bit of imagination you can turn any shoe into a face. Use whatever materials you can find and try out different skin colours. Try making the teeth and tongue from modelling clay, too.

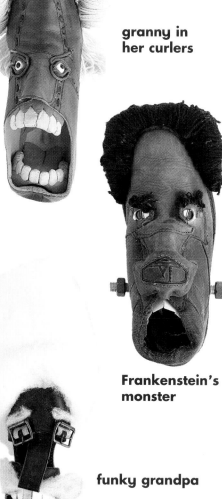

granny in her curlers

Frankenstein's monster

funky grandpa

terrible twins

BUS SHELF

YOU WILL NEED

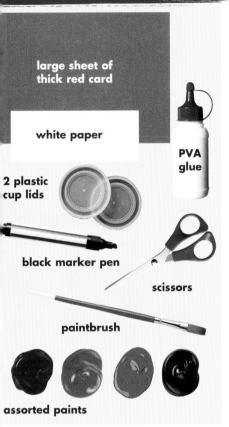

large sheet of thick red card

white paper

PVA glue

2 plastic cup lids

black marker pen

scissors

paintbrush

assorted paints

Turn a boring bookshelf into a brightly coloured bus.

BEFORE

1 First cut a bus shape from red card and cut out the windows. Make the bus 20cm bigger than your bookshelf all round.

2 Draw steps at the back of the bus with a black marker pen. Paint the cup lids black and glue them in place as wheels.

3 Decorate a strip of white paper and glue it along the side of your bus. Stick on a number sign, too.

4 Now glue the bus to one side of your bookshelf. Put things on the shelf through the bus windows.

AFTER

YOU WILL NEED

stripy black and white sock

black and white felt

googly eyes

black wool

double-sided tape

large empty tape reel

scissors

Store all those little things away in the mouth of a sock zebra. Try making a bug or even a giraffe, too.

1 First push the empty tape reel into the top of the sock.

2 Stick a length of double-sided tape along the front of the sock, from just behind the tape reel to the tip of the toe. Cut short lengths of wool and stick them across the tape to make a mane.

ears

nostrils

3

Now cut out the felt pieces for the ears and nostrils. Stick the black part of the ear to the white part using double-sided tape.

4

Pull the sock just over the tape reel to make a nose. Using small pieces of double-sided tape, stick the ears and nostrils in place. Now stick on the googly eyes. Add a few extra pieces of wool to make a funky fringe.

Use pipe cleaners and ping pong balls to make a sock bug. Bend a pipe cleaner to make the wing shape, then glue tissue paper over it.

With a yellow sock and some brown felt shapes you can make a giraffe – the sock makes a perfect long giraffe neck.

GROOVY GLITTER SHAKERS

YOU WILL NEED

- empty herb or spice pot
- red and black felt, black fur fabric and other scraps of fabric
- cotton wool
- scissors
- keyring
- PVA glue
- paintbrush
- gold, red and pink acrylic paints
- black felt-tip pen
- sequins
- gold card
- paper fasteners

Give your glitter a bit of character with these great shakers.

1 Unscrew the lid of the pot. To make the **queen** shaker, paint it gold. To make the **soldier** shaker paint it red. Paint on a pink face and draw or paint on eyes, a nose and a mouth.

2 To dress the **soldier**, cut a piece of red felt as high as the pot and wide enough to wrap right around it. Glue it to the pot, making sure the felt joins at the front, in line with the face.

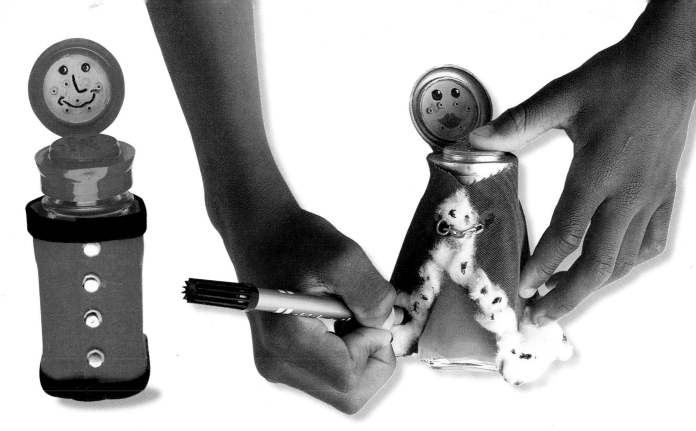

3 Cut two strips of black felt, about 1cm wide and long enough to wrap right around the pot. Glue them in place. Cut the ends off four paper fasteners, then glue them in place to make brass buttons.

4 To dress the **queen**, wrap a rectangle of fabric round to make a cloak. Glue on a cotton wool 'fur' edge and draw on some black spots. Cut the chain off the key ring and glue it on with a sequin at each end. Glue some fabric inside the cloak to make a skirt.

5 To make the **soldier's helmet**, cut a rectangle of black fur 14cm x 7cm. Wrap it round so it's just big enough to balance on the open lid of the pot. Glue it at the back.

6

To make the **queen's crown**, cut some gold card the same size as the soldier's helmet. Cut a zigzag edge around the top and add sequins and a cotton wool trim, to match the cloak, round the bottom. Now fill the pots with glitter.

If you want to shut the lids, just balance the crown or helmet on top of the closed glitter shaker.

SWEET

6 cooked pancakes

4 tablespoons strawberry or raspberry jam

½ teaspoon desiccated coconut

1 Fold each pancake in half and carefully slice it into thin strips with a sharp knife.

2 Put the shredded pancakes into a shallow bowl. Then spoon the jam into the centre to look like pasta sauce.

3 For the 'Parmesan cheese', gently sprinkle the desiccated coconut in the centre of the jam.

SPAGHETTI

Fool your friends by turning pancakes into a perfect pasta dish.

You can buy ready-made pancakes from most supermarkets, or use a pancake batter mix and follow the instructions on the packet.

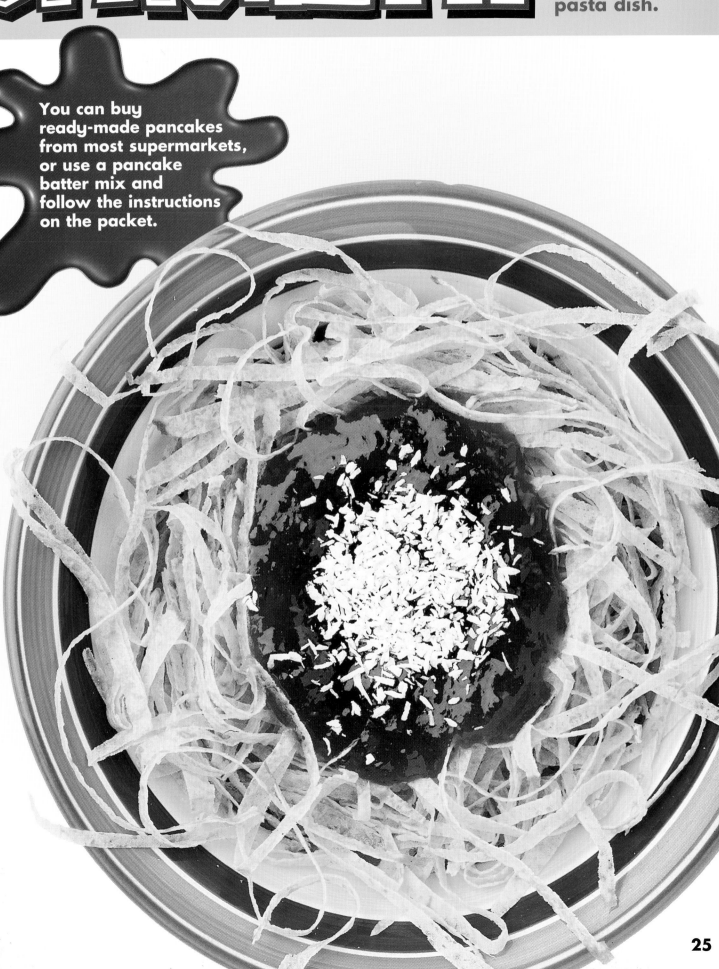

VENUS FLYTRAP

YOU WILL NEED

- black felt-tip pen
- old pencil
- paper bowl
- paper plate
- paintbrush
- scissors
- green paint
- double-sided tape
- thin red foam
- elastic band

Make a paper plant that comes alive with a snap!

1 Fold the paper **bowl** in half and cut off each corner to make a straight edge.

2 Cut zigzags along the edges of the folded bowl. Then make a cut on each side of the bowl, about 2cm up from the fold. Make each cut 1cm long.

3

Cut the foam into a tongue shape. Then cut a slit in the bowl, as long as the tongue is wide, in the centre of the fold.

4

Fold the paper **plate** in half. Copy this leaf outline onto one half, then cut around it. Cut the other side to match, making a symmetrical shape.

5

Put a piece of double-sided tape on the narrow end of the leaf. Stick the pencil on the tape and fold the plate around it.

Fold back two triangles from the top part of the plate and tape them to the back of the bowl.

6

Paint the plate and bowl green but not the teeth. Poke the tongue into the slit. Now stretch the elastic band over the bowl and slot it into the four cuts to make the flytrap snap.

STYLISH STORAGE BOXES

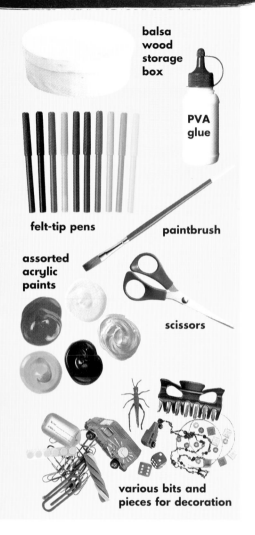

balsa wood storage box

PVA glue

felt-tip pens

paintbrush

assorted acrylic paints

scissors

various bits and pieces for decoration

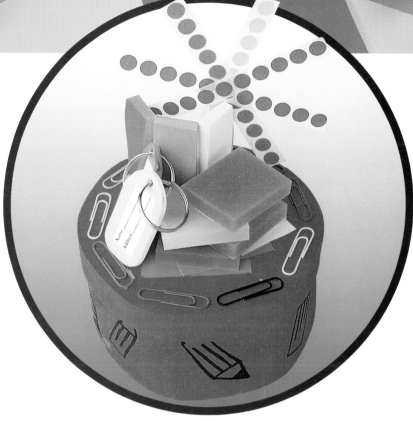

There's no limit to what you can use to decorate these handy storage boxes.

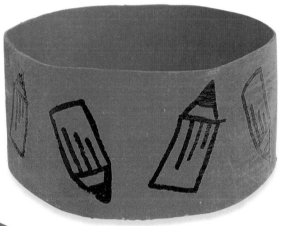

1

First decide on the theme of your box. Paint it inside and out and draw on designs using felt-tip pens.

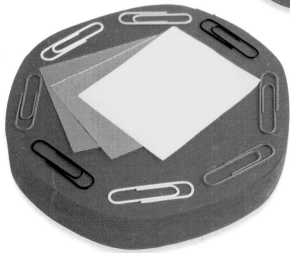

2

Now build up the sculpture on the lid. Start with a base, such as the bright paper and coloured paperclips shown here.

3

Add more items to your sculpture. Arrange them on the box lid before gluing them down to see which things fit together best.

smart ideas

Decide on a theme for your box, then find the right things to build up your sculpture.

beauty box

4

Add the finishing touches to your stylish storage box. Try gluing things to the side of the box, too.

If you can't find a plain wooden box (available from craft shops), use a cheese box. You can buy these in most supermarkets.

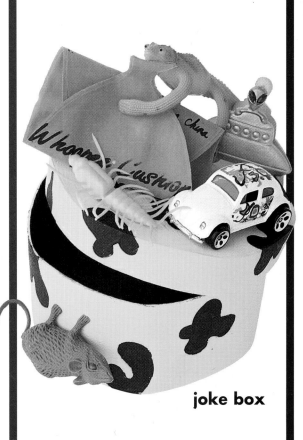

joke box

CRACKING POP-UP CARD

YOU WILL NEED

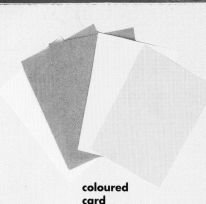

coloured
card

lolly stick

glue
stick

pencil

black felt-tip pen

tape

scissors

Make the perfect pop-up card for Easter or any other time of the year.

2 Open out one of the egg shapes and cut a small slit, as wide as the lolly stick, in the centre of the fold. Poke about 1cm of the lolly stick through the fold and tape it down.

1 Fold a sheet of yellow card in half widthways. Draw two egg shapes on one side, making sure both are exactly the same and about 14cm high. Make the flat part of the egg where the fold is. Then cut around the shapes.

3 Now take the second egg shape and glue it over the first, hiding the lolly stick.

4 Using these shapes as a template, cut out the chick's body and two wings from yellow card. Then cut two feet from brown card.

wing

body

fold here

foot

5 Cut four cracked half-shell shapes from brown card. Glue one to each side of each egg, one on the inside and one on the outside.

6 Fold each of the four legs inwards, about 1cm from the bottom, to make four tabs. Glue the tabs onto the open egg, just by the fold. Now glue the feet onto the chick, bending the claws outwards and gluing them to the egg. ⇨

7 Now glue a wing to each side of the chick. Cut a beak from orange card and glue that on too. Cut four small circles to make eyes, and glue two in place on each side of the chick. Lastly, draw on two black pupils.

8 Write a personal message on one side of the closed card.

HAPPY EASTER

love Kirsten xxx

QUICK MAKE

FUNKY FRAMES

YOU WILL NEED

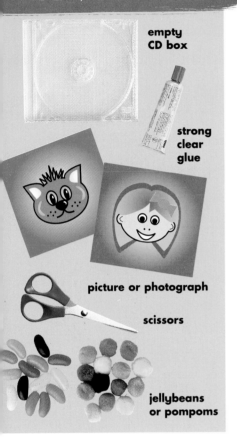

empty
CD box

strong
clear
glue

picture or photograph

scissors

jellybeans
or pompoms

Glue small objects onto an empty CD box
to turn it into a fantastic frame.

1 Find a picture or photograph
to go in the frame. Make sure
it fits perfectly by using the
CD cover as a template.

2 Slide the picture into the CD
box. Glue pompoms, jellybeans
or anything else you can find
round the edges of the box.

Put a sticky pad
on the back of
your frame to
attach it to a wall.

Coloured paper and card are some of the easiest craft materials to find and with some scissors, glue and a few felt-tip pens you can turn them into all sorts of things.

Cut a face shape from thin card, then use paper to make the features. You can bend strips of paper or curl them around a pencil to make the features on the face and hair.

To make paper or card concertinas, glue two strips together to make a right angle, then fold each strip over the other. Glue a concertina into a small decorated box to make a mini jack-in-the-box.

A short concertina makes a great pop-out snake card. Glue a snake's head made from card to one end of the concertina, and glue the other end inside the card. Draw on the rest of the snake's body or cut the triangle pattern from pieces of coloured card or paper.

Make paper mosaic pictures or cards by cutting small pieces of coloured paper. Draw a pencil outline of your design on a piece of card, then stick on the paper pieces, snipping them where necessary to fit your design.

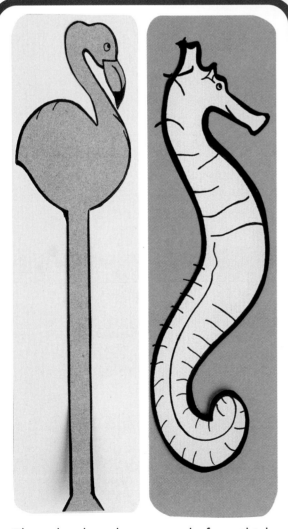

These bookmarks are made from thick card. Draw the animal design on thinner card and cut it out. Glue the top part of the animal only to the thick card – slide the book page under the part which isn't stuck down, for example the flamingo's legs.

Make a 3-D cityscape by bending pieces of corrugated card and sticking on different coloured windows. Put smaller buildings at the front and make a corrugated card sky for the backdrop.

35

FLOUR BALLOON FACES

YOU WILL NEED

large, strong balloons

empty tape reel

jug of flour

scissors

pipe cleaners

cotton wool

googly eyes with push-on backs

wool

With different coloured balloons, you can make a whole family of faces.

1

Stretch the neck of the balloon around the tape reel to make a funnel. Holding the balloon over a tray, carefully pour in the flour. Keep pressing the balloon down to push out the air and make room for as much flour as possible.

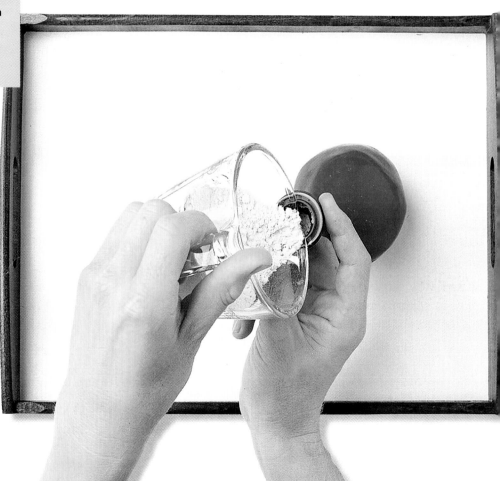

2 When the balloon is completely full, take the tape reel out, push out all the air and tie a knot in the top.

3 Push the stalk of each googly eye through the top of the balloon, just above the knot. Then push the back of the eye on to keep it in place.

4 For the hair, cut short lengths of wool and tie one piece around the middle of the bunch. Use this piece to tie it around the knot in the balloon. ⇨

Filling the balloon with flour can get messy, so hold it over a tray and pour in small amounts of flour at a time.

5 Stretch and bend your balloon face to make all sorts of expressions. Be careful not to stretch it too much in case it bursts!

Poke in a cotton wool nose or add pipe cleaner antennae to personalise each balloon face.

PENGUIN BOTTLE

YOU WILL NEED

sponge ball

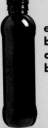
empty black drink bottle

paper bowl

black and white card

scissors

googly eyes

double-sided tape

paintbrush

black, red and yellow paint

Turn a black drink bottle or a full bottle of cola into this perky penguin.

1

Paint the sponge ball black, then tape the googly eyes in place. Use scissors to snip a hole in the bottom of the ball.

2

Paint the bowl orange (mix red and yellow together). Cut the beak shape from the curved edge and tape it onto the head. Now push the hole in the ball onto the lid of the bottle.

3

Cut an oval of white card and a triangle of black card. Tape on the white chest and black wings.

4

Cut the feet from the painted bowl. Tape them under the bottle.

round marshmallow cake

large white marshmallows

wide sweet lace

cola sweet lace

silver cake decoration balls

orange jellybean

liquorice sweets

liquorice cartwheel

SQUIDGY

1

First make the snowman's body. Place a circle of marshmallows on a board or plate. Add three more layers on top, each one smaller than the one below it.

2

To make the snowman's hat, first remove the sweet from the centre of the liquorice cartwheel. Now push two liquorice sweets into the hole.

If you can only find chocolate covered marshmallow cakes, carefully peel off the chocolate and sprinkle the cake with some desiccated coconut.

SNOWMAN

This snowman's not cold but he certainly looks cool.

3 Press a jellybean nose and silver ball eyes and a mouth into the marshmallow cake head. Carefully balance the head on top of the body and the hat on top of the head.

4 Poke small pieces of cola lace into the body to make arms. Wrap a sweet scarf around the snowman's neck, folding it over at the front.

SHOE SHOE BOX

YOU WILL NEED

- shoe box
- PVA glue
- old newspapers
- tape
- paintbrush
- blue, white and red acrylic paint
- scissors
- pencil
- white shoelaces

Store your trainers in style in this stylish trainer box.

1 Scrunch up pieces of newspaper and tape them all round the sides of the shoe box to make a trainer shape. Don't forget the round toe.

2

Mix some PVA glue with water. Dip strips of newspaper into the mixture and lay them over the scrunched up paper. Cover the whole outside of the box with two layers of paper strips. Leave to dry.

3

Cut the edges off the shoe box lid. Cut out a semicircular shape at one end. Now draw two stripes in pencil, as shown. Use a sharp pencil to poke six holes on each stripe.

4

Paint the lid to give it blue and red stripes. When the paint is dry, thread laces through the holes and tie a bow at the top. ⇨

Turn your box into any type of shoe you like. You could paint it pink for a ballet shoe – and use pink satin ribbon to add a pretty bow.

5 Paint the inside of the shoe white and copy the blue and red design on the outside. Put a strip of tape on the bottom of the lid and attach it to the front of the box to make a flap.

A coat of clear varnish or PVA glue over the paint will give your shoe shoe box a strong, shiny finish.

SHARK PEGS

YOU WILL NEED

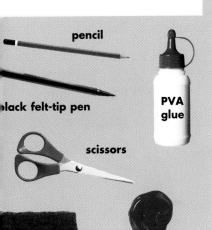

large sheet of thick white card

pencil

black felt-tip pen

PVA glue

scissors

sponge

blue, white and silver acrylic paint

Transform a plain wooden coat rail into a magnificent deep-sea creature.

BEFORE

1 Use PVA glue to stick the coat rail onto a large sheet of thick card.

2 Draw a shark shape in pencil around the coat rail. If the card isn't big enough, you can draw the fins and tail separately and glue them on.

3 Dab on blue and white paint with a sponge. Add silver highlights. Cut zigzag teeth into the mouth and draw an eye around the first peg.

AFTER

45

RUBY REINDEER

YOU WILL NEED

light brown fur fabric

strips of dark brown fur fabric

black, white and red felt

scissors

PVA glue

pipe cleaners (including two brown ones)

Wrap your hot-water bottle in a furry cover to keep out the cold.

1 Cut a rectangle of light brown fur fabric large enough to wrap right round your hot-water bottle. Glue it together at the back where it overlaps.

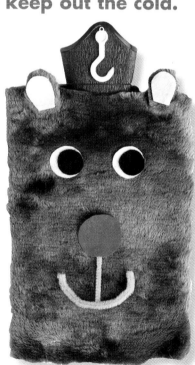

2 Now glue on the face. Add fur ears with white felt insides, black and white felt eyes and a round red felt nose. The mouth is made from two pieces of brown pipe cleaner.

3

To make the antlers, dot glue along a pipe cleaner, then wind a strip of dark brown fur around it. Don't leave any gaps. Cover four pipe cleaners like this.

4

To make each antler, twist the bottom part of two fur-covered pipe cleaners together. Now glue one antler behind each ear.

Make sure the antlers are completely covered so that no sharp pipe cleaner ends are poking out.

TIDY TRINKET BOX

YOU WILL NEED

empty chocolate box (with a tray inside)

shells, twigs, leaves, sand or any other natural materials

paintbrush

PVA glue

gold acrylic paint

This richly decorated box would make a great present for someone special.

1

First decide on your design. Lay twigs, leaves, shells, sand or anything else you can find on the lid of the chocolate box. When you are happy with your design, glue everything in place.

2

Now paint the lid gold, inside and out. Use a thin brush to make sure you get into all the gaps.

3

Next paint the bottom part of the box, inside and out, and the plastic chocolate tray. When the paint's dry, place the tray inside the box.

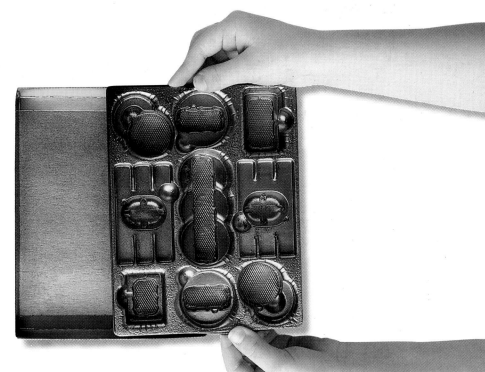

smart *ideas*

Try using different shaped boxes and a variety of other materials. Dried lentils and pasta are just some of the things glued onto this unusually shaped box and painted silver.

Using spray paint can save time, especially when painting the lid of the box.

SOCK WALRUS

YOU WILL NEED

- ping pong ball
- old grey sock
- elastic bands
- 2 lolly sticks
- dried red lentils
- paintbrush
- white paint
- soft modelling clay
- scissors
- round-headed pins
- double-sided tape

Take an old sock and turn it into this friendly walrus.

2 Drop the head into the sock so the nose is right at the end of the toe. Wind an elastic band round the sock to hold the head in place.

1 To make the head, mould a nose shape out of modelling clay and push it onto the ping pong ball.

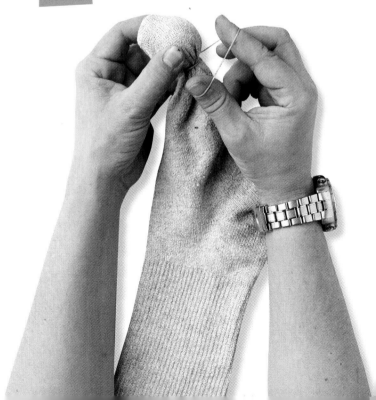

3 Cut the two shapes shown here off the end of the sock. Don't throw them away – you will need them later on.

4 Fill the sock about three quarters full of lentils. Tie another elastic band around the top of the sock to stop the lentils from spilling out.

5 Take the spare sock pieces and stick each one together with double-sided tape, leaving one end open. Bend out the open end and use double-sided tape to attach it to the walrus, making one flipper on each side.

6 Push three pins into the walrus' head to make two eyes and a nose. Paint the lolly sticks white. Using scissors, carefully make two small slits under its chin, then poke in two lolly stick tusks.

SMART IDEAS GLITTER

Use loose glitter or glitter glue pens to add sparkle to just about anything. You can buy shiny card and paper too to bring extra shine to your makes.

Cut stencils out of thick card and paint in the cut-out areas with glue. Sprinkle over loose glitter, then shake off any extra glitter to leave behind a great sparkly design.

Paint empty matchboxes and add a glitter design and sequins to make glitzy gifts. With such small designs, it can be easier to use glitter glue, but with a steady hand loose glitter can work too.

To make place cards, fold a square of card in half and write the name with glitter glue. Dab some glue around the edge of the card and sprinkle on a glitter border. Add some glitter to an extra design cut from shiny card, too.

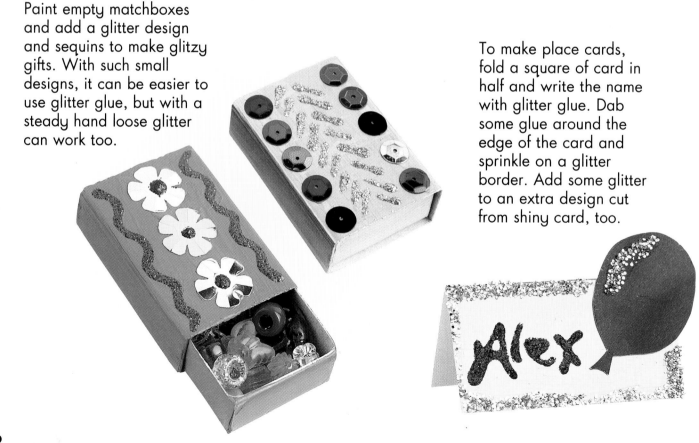

Glitter glue pens are great for adding outlines to letters or shapes cut from paper, or drawing on swirls. You might find it easier to draw the outline in pencil first, then squeeze the glitter glue over it.

Cut the basic shape of this frame from thick gold card, then glue on panels and corner shapes made from gold paper. Draw on the glitter design with a glitter glue pen, or draw with normal glue and sprinkle loose glitter over your design.

Make gift tags from pieces of shiny holographic card. Squeeze on a glitter glue design or glue on sequins. Use sparkly thread to attach your tag to the present.

53

MASQUERADE MASK

YOU WILL NEED

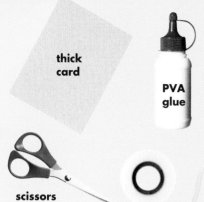

thick card

PVA glue

scissors

tape

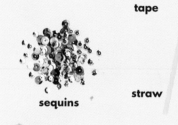

sequins

straw

feathers

glitter glue

Brighten up a fancy dress party with this multicoloured mask.

1 Trace this mask shape to make a template, then use the template to cut a mask shape from thick card.

2 Draw glitter glue outlines around the eyeholes. Now glue feathers all along the top half of the mask, making sure you don't cover the eyeholes.

3 Carefully glue sequins all over the parts of the mask not covered by feathers. Use different coloured sequins to make your own pattern.

4

Tape a straw to the back of the mask, on the right side if you're right-handed, and the left side if you're left-handed. Use the straw to hold the mask up to your face.

smart *ideas*

Use whatever materials you can find to make a themed mask, like this football one.

GHOST

125g
caster
sugar

1 teaspoon
vanilla essence

125g
butter

150g
plain
flour

1½ tablespoons
cocoa powder

cocktail stick

elastic

1 Cream the butter and sugar together with a wooden spoon. Add the vanilla essence, then stir in the flour. Divide the mixture in half and roll one half into a blunt-ended sausage, about 15cm long and 4cm wide. Mix the cocoa powder into the other half.

2 Wrap both halves of dough in clingfilm and refrigerate for about an hour. Then unwrap the plain dough and carefully cut a V shape out of each side, to make the ghost shape.

3 Now unwrap the cocoa dough. Break off two pieces and roll them into thin sausages. Use them to fill in the V shapes, as shown.

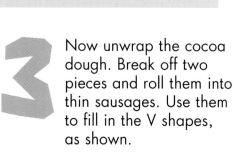

4 Lightly dust the kitchen surface with cocoa powder, then roll the remaining cocoa dough into a rectangle big enough to wrap round the plain dough. Roll it round and refrigerate, wrapped in clingfilm, for an hour.

BISCUITS

6

Use a cocktail stick to mark out eyes, a mouth and a hole so you can hang your biscuits up on a piece of elastic.

5 Unwrap the dough and slice it into eight thin pieces. Put the biscuits onto a lightly greased baking tray.

7 Ask an adult to help you bake your biscuits in a preheated oven at 180°C/350°F/gas mark 4 for 10-12 minutes. Leave them to cool before threading a piece of elastic through them and hanging them up.

To make jellybean ghosts, wrap a small handful of jellybeans in a square of white fabric. Tie some elastic round to keep them in place. Draw on a face and hang the ghost up.

BATTY BAT

YOU WILL NEED

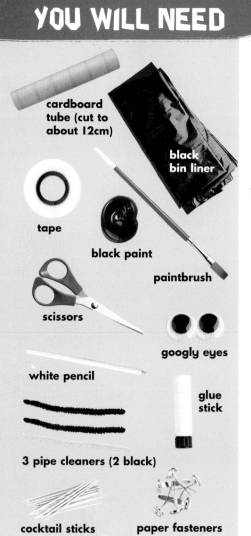

cardboard tube (cut to about 12cm)

black bin liner

tape

black paint

paintbrush

scissors

googly eyes

white pencil

glue stick

3 pipe cleaners (2 black)

cocktail sticks

paper fasteners

If you've got the right materials hanging around, why not turn them into this batty bat?

2 Paint the tube black and tape the two legs inside. Now gently bend in the bottom of the tube on both sides.

1 To make each leg, bend a zigzag at the end of a pipe cleaner, as shown here. Now squeeze it together to make three claws.

58

3 Using a white pencil, draw a V shape at the top of the tube. Carefully cut along the two white lines.

Now bend down the top of the tube. The cut out V should lift up to make the bat's mouth.

4 To make the nose, push a paper fastener through the point of the V shape, so that the round part is on top. Bend the two pins underneath to look like fangs. Now glue a googly eye to the tube, either side of the mouth.

5 Next make the wings. Cut two rectangles from the bin liner, 30cm x 16cm. Lay one rectangle flat and glue eight cocktail sticks to it, in two groups of four, as shown. Now glue a pipe cleaner in place between the two groups of cocktail sticks.

make this gap about 3cm

6 Glue the second rectangle of bin liner over the first. Cut around the cocktail sticks and pipe cleaner to make this wing shape. ⇨

7 To finish off your bat, glue the wings to the body. Bend the pipe cleaner claws to help your bat grip as it hangs upside down.

Make a whole family of bats! You could make baby bats by using small round sweet tubes.